The Small Business Tax Guide - To Health Care

Crystal Stranger, EA

DEDICATION

This book is dedicated to everyone out there who needs health care and to the employers who will provide it.

CONTENTS

Introduction   7

1   Affordable Care   9
   Act Basics

2   ACA Issues for   13
   Individuals

3   Required Employee   23
   Coverage

4   Small Business   33
   Health Care Tax
   Credit

5   Net Investment   41
   Income Tax

6   Deductions   57

7   Employees   79

8   Depreciation   91

9   Sold!   99

INTRODUCTION

Although I've not been a proponent of the Affordable Care Act (ACA), aka "Obamacare", the idea of providing health care to everyone in the country is one I've always been in favor of. I think there should be a "fall-back" system that as a society we provide food, shelter and access to health care for those in need, preferably with guidance to help them get independent again. This may be a step in that direction, only time will tell. What is obvious though is what a logistical nightmare it has been for everyone involved, the IRS, accountants, and most significantly, the taxpayers affected by it.

Tax season has just started for the first year the ACA comes fully into effect, and the tax industry has been paralyzed by the new demands. Our software is not yet ready to handle the intricacies involved, and there is a high likelihood that many returns filed now will need to be amended in the future as the laws seem to be changing on a daily basis.

As this is a rapidly changing area of tax law, portions of this book then may be outdated by the time you read it. But hopefully the information contained within will still be of benefit and guide you in the right direction to find the information you need. However, if you have a complicated situation regarding ACA I would highly recommend working with a competent tax advisor when filing your return. OK, now that I have gotten the required disclaimer out of the way let us delve into the basics of the ACA.

Affordable Care Act Basics

Affordable Care?

Intentions are often better than the realities they create. The "Patient Protection and Affordable Care Act" was signed into law by president Barrack Obama on March 23, 2010. The goal of this law was to increase the quality and affordability of health care in the United States.

Certainly many people who had been denied insurance for pre-exising conditions have benefited from being able to obtain insurance, which is a blessing in their lives I am sure. I must admit though to taking a bit of offence at the central cornerstone of ACA being the purchase of insurance policies. My experiences with big insurers such as Blue Cross and Kaiser have left me less than pleased. The bottom line is I've never felt they have their patients best interests in mind. But luckily small businesses have the option of self-insuring which can be both money saving and provide better care options to their employees.

There are many issues with ACA, especially for employers, but also many benefits. The small business health care credit is a double-dipping credit, meaning you can get both a credit and a deduction on the same expenditure, reducing your costs greatly depending on your tax bracket.

The ACA provisions are being gradually phased in. The first provisions came in 2010 by offering credits to employers offering health insurance to certain employees. Now for the 2014 tax year the full requirements for employee health plan offerings and credits from the SHOP marketplace plans are in play.

The main part of the ACA I dislike is that it forces everyone to buy plans through the existing insurance companies. This frustrates me on a concerned citizen level as I don't think the medical insurance companies in the US have the best interests of their patients in mind at most times. Also most of these plans that are being offered have such high deductibles and out of pocket costs that they are just not as good of value to consumers as the plans offered prior to ACA. Self-insuring and better plans are options, but most employees will now have these plans that cover only 60% of the cost of medical care. Potentially this could still lead to large medical debt for individuals.

Also the implementation has been poorly organized, causing a nightmare for many employers and employees alike. The federal government has left it up to the states to form marketplaces for both individuals and businesses to buy insurance, and the differences from state to state are staggering.

In this book I will first cover the specifics for individuals briefly, as some self-employed individuals or those who have small businesses may fall into the range where they will be affected by the individual penalties and credits. Then I will delve into the requirements on businesses to provide health care. Later we will cover the Small Business Health Care Credit and all that entails. At the end I will touch on the Net Investment Income Tax and how that can affect you when selling your business.

ACA Issues for Individuals

The Great Social Cost

The cost of insuring the masses must fall on the shoulders of the masses, so one major component of the ACA is the penalties that taxpayers will start having to pay on their individual returns. If taxpayers are not covered by an insurance plan or eligible for one of the exemptions they will be fined on their tax return for not carrying insurance.

This can affect small business owners who are not required to provide insurance for their employees. As the penalty is based on gross income this can become quite a high penalty tax to pay in a year where you get a sudden windfall or sell a business, so is something to plan well for. Also many of the exemptions are not available when filing the status Married Filing Separate, so if you are going through a divorce you may also end up getting dinged.

Penalties

The Individual Shared Responsibility Payment is a very sweet and socialistic way of stating "Penalty Tax". This rule taxes every individual who does not meet one of the exceptions I will cover in the next part. In 2014 this is a minimum penalty of $95 per person, or 1% of adjusted gross income, which ever is greater. This amount will rise to $695 or 2.5% of gross income in years after 2015, with inflation adjustments written into the law. This amount is capped at the national average for Bronze coverage, or $2,448 for 2014 for an individual, $12,240 for a family of five or more.

The penalties will apply for all dependents you claim if they do not meet the minimum coverage rule. So for some taxpayers it may be worth asking if it is worth claiming a dependent in a year when the ACA penalties may apply.

Tax Tip: Choosing not to claim a dependent on your tax return may create tax savings if subject to a Individual Shared Responsibility Payment.

Minimum Essential Coverage

The IRS considers most individual, employer and government plans to meet the conditions of Minimum Essential Coverage (MEC), at least for the 2014 tax year. This includes any medical plan you have purchased directly from an insurance company. So if you had insurance prior to

ACA you are covered, unless the insurance only covered specific items, such as medical or vision policies.

It is also good to note that AfterCorps and AmeriCorps plans do not meet the MEC requirements. And starting in 2015 Medicare plans that are specifically for pregnancy, family planning or emergency services will no longer qualify. Also in 2015 higher education institutions that offer plans directly will need to be recognized individually by HHS in order for their plans to qualify.

U.S. Citizens who are foreign residents do not need to maintain MEC. However, all residents of the U.S., even legal resident aliens are subject to ACA. Remember that everyone in your household must be insured, or meet the foreign residence test to qualify.

Tax Tip: If you lived outside of the US you do not need to meet the Minimum Essential Coverage requirements.

Exemptions

There are also a number of exemptions that may allow you to not have to pay the Individual Shared Responsibility Payment. However, getting these exemptions means applying for them from the marketplace and being issued a certificate that shows you are exempt.

The following is a list of common exemptions:

- **Unaffordable coverage** – The cost for the least expensive employer-sponsored or Marketplace insurance is more than eight percent of household income for the year.
- **Short coverage gap** – For less than three consecutive months without coverage during the year.
- **Household Income below Filing Threshold** – For if household income is below the minimum threshold for filing a tax return.

- **Certain Non-Citizens** – For those who were neither a U.S. citizen, U.S. national, nor an alien lawfully present in the U.S.
- **Members of a Health Care Sharing Ministry** – For members of a a tax-exempt organization whose members share a common set of ethical or religious beliefs and have shared medical expenses continuously since at least December 31, 1999.
- **Members of Indian Tribes** – For members of a federally- recognized Indian tribe, or eligible for services through an Indian health care provider or the Indian Health Service.
- **Incarceration** – For those in a jail, prison, or similar penal institution or correctional facility.
- **Members of Certain Religious Sects** – For members of religious sects in existence since December 31, 1950, and recognized by the SSA as conscientiously opposed to insurance benefits.

So now that you understand what you are up against with the exemptions, how do you make use of them? That gets more complex as some exemptions require a certificate from the marketplace, whereas others can be taken directly on your tax return. Form 8965 is the form where all the magic takes place, so if this applies to you I would highly suggest reading the instructions for this form and getting familiar with what information you need to ask for.

Since the policies purchased through the exchange are priced based on an estimated income level, if you purchase a policy through this exchange you may end up with a refund or a balance due at the end of the year. Can be a confusing and potentially costly process for self employed taxpayers who don't usually know how much their adjusted gross income will be until they have filed their taxes come year end.

Required Employee Coverage

The Great Debate

I'm convinced there must be a lot of mid-size companies out there that determined it was cheaper to lobby congress to adjust the laws than to pay health insurance for their employees. The regulations for who is considered a small business exempt from paying for employee coverage has been the hot debate since the ACA was first signed in. It seems a weekly occurrence that a new bill is spearheaded to shave an edge off here or there.

This week's amusing tidbit was the "Hire More Heroes Act" which was the first law signed in by the senate in 2015. This law supposedly creates jobs by exempting Veterans from being counted as employees so as not to trigger the requirement to provide coverage to other employees. It seems doubtful that this bill will create new jobs, but rather will let certain companies not have to cover their other employees with health insurance. Just a tidy little loophole that probably helped some pipeline companies not have to pay health insurance for their hard working laborers.

I can certainly understand the desire to not want to pay taxes, but isn't providing employee health care usually a good thing? Having benefits at a job gives employees a good incentive to stick around, and makes changing jobs a bit trickier. I can understand companies who pay minimum wage not wanting to provide this, but they usually won't have to as their workers earn so little that they fall under the poverty level exemptions.

Employer Shared Responsibility Payments

At the crux of this issue is the Employer Shared Responsibility Payments. Much like their insidious friends on the individual side of the spectrum, the employer shared responsibility payments can add up to significant penalty taxes if not properly managed. This comes into play with that magic 50 Full Time Equivalent(FTE) employee number, in which part time employees count as half- so you could essentially have up to 100 part time employees and be considered as having 50 FTE.

The danger in the Employer Shared Responsibility Payments is with how they are calculated. If an employer with 50 or more employees does not offer affordable minimum coverage insurance to all of their full time employees, and any full time employee claims a tax credit from an insurance policy bought from the Marketplace, all hell breaks loose. The Employer Shared Responsibility Payment in this situation is the number of full time employees, minus up to 30 employees, then multiplied by $2,000 each. This means for an employer of 50 employees where one full time employee claimed a credit will owe a whopping $40,000 in penalty tax!

Part time employees, meaning those who work less than 30 hours per week, count as half of a full time employee. So with this calculation you could have up to 100 part time employees before having to pay. Seasonal employees who work less than 120 days in the year are not counted as employees for these purposes. Also new hires are not required to be covered for their first 90 days.

Now we're starting to see where the lobbyists pay off. Still I don't really see the problem though, just give the kids insurance already. There is a safe harbor law in the ruling where if the plans offered have premiums of less than 9.5% of the poverty level for the employee to pay, that even if they claim a credit for buying through the marketplace, the employer won't be subject to the Shared Responsibility Payment.

While the penalties are severe, there are a lot of exceptions. Plus the starting year for these provisions has been pushed back from 2014 to 2015, and even for the 2015 tax year there are transitional relief that will be coming into play, with employers of more than 50 but less than 100 full time employees still being considered exempt.

Large Employers

Companies with more than 50 FTE employees, the IRS has deemed Large Employers subject to additional reporting rules. If a company is part of a group of companies such as a parent and subsidiary that meet the FTE number combined, they all are considered large employers under this rule.

Form 1095-C will need to be filed for each employee covered under the plan, and given out in a similar way to W-2s or other information returns. Then form 1094-C will need to be filed on behalf of the company. These forms are still in draft form as of now, but look rather straightforward except for self-insurers.

The main problem with this reporting method is the need to determine who amongst a large employer's workforce are full and part time employees, leading to the offering of alternate methods of reporting. The first regards issuing a statement to employees in IRS format by January 31 following the year of coverage. The second is a full exemption of reporting requirements. If insurance is offered to at least 98% of employees no reporting will be needed.

Everyone has been complaining incessantly about how convoluted these rules are. Therefore the IRS has offered transitional relief for this year and the enforcement of these rules have been pushed off at least one more year, scheduled to start being required in the 2015 tax year.

Self-Insurance Loophole

Large companies have self-insured for decades. This can now be a good choice also for small and mid-size companies who fall into the range where the employer shared responsibility payments come into play. For employers with at least 30-50 employees they may find self-insurance to be a less expensive option than purchasing policies through the individual exchanges.

For employers with a young and healthy workforce this can be a much less expensive way to provide benefits. Generally employers who go this direction buy reinsurance for a stop loss coverage, usually in the range of $20,000 to $50,000. This means if an employee comes down with cancer or needs hospitalization the cost for the employer is limited. Also insurance companies like Blue Cross offer management services to process claims and for employees under this arrangement it appears just like a normal insurance plan.

There is some controversy surrounding this now as insurance has found that selling these plans are a loophole for them to increase their profit beyond the restrictions placed in the ACA. Also there are concerns that this will weaken the SHOP marketplace becoming established. California has already taken steps to put legislation in limiting the ability of companies to self insure. Under the proposed legislation there would be a stop-loss trigger of no reinsurance plans below $95,000 allowed.

One additional facet to Self-Insuring is that there is a payment due to support the government's trust fund for Patient Centered Outcomes. This is minimal however, the payments due are currently $2.08 per life covered by your insurance plan. So if you had 100 employees with another 80 dependents on your plan, you would owe a total of $374.40. Not exactly a bank-breaker.

The Bureaucratic Rat's Nest

The IRS is a mess right now. The other provisions of the ACA are tough enough to enforce that the IRS seems frozen as to how to handle the Employer Shared Responsibility Payment. The most recent announcement is that there will be no tax forms used to calculate if a payment is due. Rather the IRS will compare tax returns filed by employees by those with employers and send letters out to demand information whenever the employees claim a credit in the marketplace. What a cluster that will be.

As these rules keep shifting and morphing, it seems like less and less businesses will be subject to the Employer Shared Responsibility Payment. However, the money to subsidize the medical industry will need to come from somewhere, so this may trigger increases in other ACA related taxes over time.

Small Business Health Care Tax Credit

The Silver Lining

It is a rare occurrence in the tax world when a new credit is released that benefits small businesses, and then the laws continue to get loosened and become more beneficial. But this is exactly what has happened with the Small Business Health Care Tax Credit provisions of the ACA. What was a 35% tax credit for years 2010-2013 has now grown to be a 50% credit! Plus this credit allows for double-dipping, meaning you can take both a credit and a deduction for the same expense paid.

So for those who have decided to accept the new laws as they are rather than fighting the government, this the icing on the cake. Not to mention that fighting the government is rarely worthwhile, too expensive, and time consuming, unless you happen to be a lawyer. For me, I'm not a lawyer, just an Enrolled Agent who has learned to find ways to read into the existing laws and find the best strategies to benefit my clients.

This means you have to play within the rules, or manipulate your business structures in such a way as to play within the rules. Between the employer health coverage payment requirements and this juicy credit the next years we will probably see a number of firms re-organizing their companies by breaking apart each piece of the business into smaller enterprises.

For example, if you owned a company that manufactures and installs counter tops the installation side of the business could be spun off into a subsidiary. This way the high commissions of the sales staff wouldn't stop the installation crew employees from qualifying for the credit.

Of course, these types of decisions can't be based on tax savings alone, they must have legitimate business purposes, and must have different owners/investors or they will fall under the "Common Control" clause in the tax code. This example's subsidiary spin-off would make sense from a business perspective as the activities and expenditures are so different between both businesses. Also by separating payroll the sales staff could likely then be switched to statutory employees, saving the company on payroll taxes.

Credit Eligibility

Qualifying for this credit takes a bit of pre-planning, meaning you can't just go file your taxes and hope you will qualify. The law states that for 2014 tax years and beyond the policy you offer to employees must have been purchased through the Small Business Health Options Marketplace, colloquially known as SHOP. There are some exceptions to this rule, and especially as many states do not yet have fully functional SHOP marketplaces this has not been enforced yet and this requirement has been pushed forward another year. But if you are considering adding a plan to cover your employees it is imperative the plan you offer is part of this system. SHOP marketplace plans are offered by most insurance brokers now, so finding this type of plan shouldn't be too difficult.

To be eligible for the credit you must cover at least 50% of the payments for eligible employees only, not for their families or dependents. Also you must offer affordable coverage to all eligible full time employees, offering coverage to part time employees is optional.

You must also have less than 25 Full time equivalent employees who earn an averaged salary of less than $50,000. What does this mean in English? Employees who work more than 30 hours per week are considered full time. Those who work between 20 and 29 hours per week are considered part time. Two part time employees are equivalent to one full time employee. And employees who work less than 20 hours per week just don't count at all towards the averages.

Seasonal workers also don't count towards the equation. What exactly is defined as seasonal workers? If someone works less than 120 days in the year they are not considered employees for health care coverage purposes for that year.

Calculating the Credit

The credit is calculated using form 8941 and the maximum credit is for wages of $25,000 a year and ten FTE employees. The credit works on a sliding scale basis for any employer with more employers or wages than that amount, decreasing the credit.

> *Tax Tip: The maximum 50% is available to employers with less than ten full time employees who pay their workers $12.50 per hour maximum wages.*

Of course, these credit limitations don't speak well for creating a living wage in the US. As with most tax laws, they reward companies in lower cost parts of the country. Still if you have a relatively low-skilled worker pool you may find yourself in the range for maxing out this credit.

Pre-2014 Credits

If you paid insurance for your employees during the years 2010 through 2013 you may be eligible for a credit of 35% of the premiums you paid in those years. Many tax preparers did not understand the laws and who this applied to, but any insurance plan over those years will qualify if your employees meet the income range and number of employees as listed above.

To claim the credit you may be able to file an amended return and you can carry the credit forward to the current year in many cases, although you can't claim a refund for more than three years from when the tax return was filed or two years after the tax was paid, whichever was later. This means if you would qualify for a credit for the 2011 or 2012 tax year you should file an amended return ASAP!

Tax Tip: You may be able to file an amended return to claim tax credit of up to 35% of what was paid for employee health insurance premiums in years 2010 through 2013.

As this is a refundable credit you may be able to treat it as a payment to offset Social Security for self-employed individuals, or receive it back as cash. This type of credit

can be so valuable, so take advantage of it
if you can.

Net Investment Income Tax

Taking a Bite

Someone has to pay for all the good provisions of the ACA, like covering uninsured people and paying for the credits. The way this was balanced out, beyond the shared responsibility payments, was by imposing two tax increases: a Medicare tax increase of 0.9% on employee compensation over $200,000 (haven't yet heard anyone crying about that one), and implementing a new 3.8% tax on passive income over certain income thresholds, known as the Net Investment Income Tax.

I've already seen this tax be quite a problem for my clients. Why? Because this tax comes in at the bottom of the tax return where self-employment taxes live and most other credits do not offset against this. Meaning you can have zero tax liability, and still owe this tax.

Will I Owe This Tax?

The key about this tax is it is triggered by Modified Adjusted Gross Income (MAGI), meaning many things that normally will reduce your Adjusted Gross Income (AGI) such as the Foreign Earned Income Exclusion, will still count as income for the Net Investment Income Tax. This is especially likely to happen in a year of high capital gains, such as when you sell your business.

The following is a chart of the income levels when this comes into play:

Filing Status	Threshold Amount
Married filing jointly	$250,000
Married filing separately	$125,000
Single	$200,000
Head of household (with qualifying person)	$200,000
Qualifying widow(er) with dependent child	$250,000

It is important to note that the IRS has stated these threshold amounts are not going to be indexed for inflation. Every year more and more people are going to start seeing this tax show up on their returns. And it often will be most noticeable in the year of a large gain, such as when selling real estate or a business.

When in that income range the tax is based on the lesser of the amount of passive income or the amount the total income passes the threshold. So, for example, if you are single and your earned income was $100,000 in a year and you sold a house with $200,000 in passive gains you will only have to pay the 3.8% additional tax on the amount your tax exceeded the threshold, or $3,800, not the full amount of passive income.

Passive Income

As the Net Investment Income Tax only taxes passive income the question then is, what is considered passive income? Interest, dividends, capital gains, rental and royalty income are all clear examples of passive income. Collectibles are also considered passive income and the 3.8% is tacked on to the already high 28% on sales of collectibles such as art or classic cars. Many annuities are passive income, unless they are part of a qualified retirement plan.

Income from businesses involved in trading of financial instruments or commodities are considered passive. And businesses that are passive activities to the taxpayer are also considered passive income. Or a recapture of basis from a passive loss when selling a limited partnership, where no income was received but past losses have lowered basis producing a phantom gain. These all can be considered passive gains subject to the Net Investment Income Tax.

What does this mean to you as a business owner? Those S-corp dividends that have always saved you from self-employment tax may now suddenly have the Net Investment Income Tax tacked on instead. Luckily you can't have both Self-employment Tax and Net Investment Income Tax on the same income, but they both are essentially the same in being a painful bottom line tax.

When you sell your business, the gain may or may not be subject to the Net Investment Income Tax. If you sell a partnership or sole proprietorship you are in the clear as the IRS has deemed this sale to not be subject to the Net Investment Income Tax, beyond what the sale of assets would be.

The regulations on this issue are still a bit unclear, and it will be interesting to see how this holds up in tax court, but I would say right now that partnerships, sole proprietorships, and S-corps can be sold without being subject to the Net Income Investment Tax. This is of course assuming you were an active partner or shareholder, and not just an investor in the company. There have been several high profile instances of tech companies converting to S-corp status before sale so the founders of the companies are not liable for Net Investment Income Tax.

Reducing the Tax

What can be done about this tax? Well, the first thing to note is that it is a "net" tax, meaning you can deduct any expenses such as brokerage fees and investment income that normally would only be deductible as part of your Itemized Deductions against this tax. Many tax advisors don't know this, so it may be wise to take a second look at any Net Investment Income Tax you paid in the past and see if you had expenses that could have reduced your tax.

Tax Tip: All your expenses related to passive income that normally would only be listed as miscellaneous itemized deductions can be deducted to reduce the Net Investment Income Tax. This can reduce your tax considerably if you have expenses that can't be used to calculate gross income.

If you are selling something large in a year, such as a piece of real estate other than your home, you may wish to use a section 1031 exchange to roll the investment in one business property that is sold into a new business property. Using this set of rules the IRS considers it as if you traded your property directly for a bigger one, and considers that reinvestment qualified for tax-deferral. The property traded for must be similar, such as investment real estate for other investment real estate, or one business for another business. If your property qualifies and you follow all the rules of the sale you can defer all tax, including any Net Investment Income Tax that would have been due.

Conclusion

While adjusting to a new and complex system can be painful, hopefully the growth from the experience and new services the ACA creates will be beneficial to all. Yes, our country is founded on principals of freedom and escape from taxation, but the first tax was passed by congress within months of ratifying the Bill of Rights. This law created an excise tax on whisky and led to our first civil war, the whisky rebellion of 1791. Tax has always been a hotly debated issue in the U.S. and always will be.

However, the idea of providing accessible medical care to all transcends the normal spectrum of taxes and laws.

Whatever side of this debate your beliefs may lie, as a business owner your interests will be best served by having good people working for you. The people of your organization are the ones who make your organization great, right? You can't deny that good people like to work for companies where they feel they are treated well, and this includes having their needs such as health insurance provided for. Plus losing one's insurance is a big deterrent for wanting to change jobs.

The bottom line is every business owner will do what is best for their bottom line. I hope in this book I have given you some new ways to improve your profit while keeping up with the demands of the ACA. Remember that embracing change is always more profitable than fighting against it.

Resources

IRS Information

Internal Revenue Service. (2014). *Questions and Answers on reporting of Offers of Health Care Coverage by Employers (Section 6056).* Available: http://www.irs.gov/Affordable-Care-Act/Employers/ Questions-and-Answers-on-Reporting-of-Offers-of-Health-Insurance-Coverage-by-Employers-Section-6056. Last accessed 1st Feb 2015.

Internal Revenue Service. (2015). *Questions and Answers on Employee Shared Responsibility Payments Under the Affordable Care Act.* Available: http://www.irs.gov/Affordable-Care-Act/Employers/ Questions-and-Answers-on-Employer-Shared-Resp onsibility-Provisions-Under-the-Affordable-Care-Act. Last accessed 15th Jan 2015.

Internal Revenue Service. (2014). *Instructions for form 8941.* Available:
http://www.irs.gov/pub/irs-pdf/i8941.pdf. Last accessed 31st Jan 2015.

Internal Revenue Service. (2014). *Small Business Health Care Tax Credit for Small Employers.* Available:
http://www.irs.gov/uac/Small-Business-Health-Car e-Tax-Credit-for-Small-Employers. Last accessed 31st Jan 2015.

Internal Revenue Service. (2014). *Patient-Centered Outcomes Research Trust Fund Fee (IRC 4375, 4376 and 4377): Questions and Answers, Affordable Care Act Provision 6301* Available:
http://www.irs.gov/uac/Patient-Centered-Outcomes -Research-Trust-Fund-Fee:-Questions-and-Answers . Last accessed 1st Feb 2015 .

Internal Revenue Service. (2013). *Internal Revenue Bulletin 2013-51*:
http://www.irs.gov/irb/2013-51_IRB/ar09.html Last accessed 31st Jan 2015.

Internal Revenue Service. (2015). *Topic 559- Net Investment Income Tax.*
Available:http://www.irs.gov/taxtopics/tc559.html. Last accessed 1st Feb 2015.

Additional Resources

Employer Information Reporting:

The Federal Register. (2014). *Information Reporting by Applicable Large Employers on Health Insurance Coverage Offered Under Employer-Sponsored Plans.* Available: https://www.federalregister.gov/articles/2014/03/10/2014-05050/information-reporting-by-applicable-large-employers-on-health-insurance-coverage-offered-under#h-27. Last accessed 1st Feb 2015.

SHOP Marketplace:

HealthCare.gov. (2014). *Small Business Health Insurance Plans.* Available: https://www.healthcare.gov/small-businesses/employers/ Last Accessed 1st Feb 2015.

Net Investment Income Tax:

The Federal Register (2013). *Net Investment Income Tax.* Available: https://www.federalregister.gov/articles/2013/12/02/2013-28410/net-investment-income-tax. Last accessed 1st Feb 2015.

ABOUT THE AUTHOR

Crystal Stranger, President of 1st Tax and the author of *The Small Business Tax Guide* (Clear Advantage, 2014), is not your average accountant by any means. As a teen she was involved in automotive racing and observed that most of the successful racers had the money and freedom to race by owning businesses. She founded several internet companies with moderate success, then switched her focus to real estate. She read every book in the library on investment while working three jobs and living in a seventeen foot trailer to save money, officially homeless. Within a year she saved a down payment, leveraged through investing in stocks, and bought her first house at the age of 21. By 26 she was a millionaire, owning several businesses and a large real estate portfolio.

Crystal's interest in tax arose when nobody could give clear answers about how much tax she would owe when selling her properties. This led her to taking a tax course to gain general knowledge, then into an educational program for becoming an Enrolled Agent. After another couple years of work and study she finally had her answers; in the process amassing an extensive knowledge in investment and small business tax laws. Crystal conceived 1st Tax as a way of sharing this specialized knowledge with those who would most benefit, by providing an online source for small business tax services.

Index

A

accountants, **8**
advisors, **47**
affordability, **10**
aftercorps, **17**
aliens, **17**
amended, **9, 39**
americorps, **17**
annuities, **44**
assets, **46**

B

bureaucratic, **31**

C

calculation, **26**
citizen, **12, 19**
citizens, **17, 19**
collectibles, **44**

commodities, **45**
compensation, **41**
congress, **23, 49**
consumers, **12**
costly, **20**
coverage, **16, 18, 23-25, 28-29, 34, 36-37**

D

deduct, **46**
deductibles, **12**
deduction, **11, 34**
deductions, **47**
deferral, **48**
dividends, **44-45**

E

education, **17**
eligibility, **35**
eligible, **14, 19, 36, 38**
employee, **11, 23-27, 29, 37, 39, 41**
employees, **11-13, 15, 23-31, 35-39**
employer, **16, 18, 25-26, 28-29, 31, 34, 37**
employers, **11, 13, 27, 29, 31, 37-38**
employment, **42, 45**
enforcement, **28**
enterprises, **34**
estate, **43, 47-48**
excise, **49**

exclusion, **42**
exempt, **18-19, 23, 27**
exemptions, **14-15, 18, 20, 24**
expenditure, **11**
expenditures, **35**

G

government, **13, 16, 30, 34**

F

facility, **19**
federally, **19**

H

hospitalization, **29**
household, **17-19, 43**

I

incarceration, **19**
incentive, **24**
inflation, **16, 43**
information, **9, 20,
   27, 31**
installation, **34-35**
institution, **19**
institutions, **17**
insurers, **11, 28**
investment, **13,
   41-42, 44-48**
investor, **46**
investors, **35**
itemized, **47**

J

jointly, **43**

L

laborers, **24**
legislation, **30**
liability, **42**
lobby, **23**
lobbyists, **26**
logistical, **8**
loophole, **24, 29-30**

M

marketplace, **12, 18, 20, 25-26, 30-31, 36**
marketplaces, **13, 36**
medicare, **17, 41**
methods, **28**

O

options, **11-12, 36**
organization, **19, 50**
outcomes, **30**

P

partnership, **45**
partnerships, **46**
payroll, **35**
penalties, **13-16, 27**
penalty, **15, 25-26**
preparers, **38**
proprietorship, **45**
proprietorships, **46**
provisions, **11, 27, 31, 33, 41**

R

recapture, **45**
refund, **20, 39**

refundable, **39**
reinsurance, **29-30**
reinvestment, **48**
requirement, **24, 36**
requirements, **11,
    13, 17-18, 28,
    34**
residence, **17**
responsibility,
    **15-16, 18, 25,
    27, 29, 31, 41**
restrictions, **30**
retirement, **44**

status, **15, 43, 46**
statutory, **35**
subsidize, **31**

T

taxation, **49**
taxpayer, **45**
taxpayers, **8, 14,
    16, 20**
threshold, **19,
    43-44**
thresholds, **42**
transitional, **27-28**

S

salary, **36**
seasonal, **26, 37**
senate, **24**
shareholder, **46**
software, **9**

workers, **24, 37-38**
workforce, **28-29**

U

uninsured, **41**

V

veterans, **24**
vision, **17**

W

whisky, **49**
worker, **38**

www.ingramcontent.com/pod-product-compliance
Lightning Source LLC
Chambersburg PA
CBHW070826210326
41520CB00011B/2130